The National Poetry Series was established in 1978 to ensure the publication of five collections of poetry annually through five participating publishers. Publication is funded annually by the Lannan Foundation, Amazon Literary Partnership, Barnes & Noble, the Poetry Foundation, the PG Family Foundation and the Betsy Community Fund, Joan Bingham, Mariana Cook, Stephen Graham, Juliet Lea Hillman Simonds, William Kistler, Jeffrey Ravetch, Laura Baudo Sillerman, and Margaret Thornton. For a complete listing of generous contributors to the National Poetry Series, please visit www.nationalpoetryseries.org.

2015 COMPETITION WINNERS

Not on the Last Day, but on the Very Last
by Justin Boening of Iowa City, IA
Chosen by Wayne Miller, to be published by Milkweed Editions

The Wug Test
by Jennifer Kronovet of New York, NY
Chosen by Eliza Griswold, to be published by Ecco

Scriptorium
by Melissa Range of Appleton, WI
Chosen by Tracy K. Smith, to be published by Beacon Press

Trébuchet
by Danniel Schoonebeek of Brooklyn, NY
Chosen by Kevin Prufer, to be published by University of Georgia Press

The Sobbing School
by Joshua Bennett of Yonkers, NY
Chosen by Eugene Gloria, to be published by Penguin

NOT ON THE
LAST DAY,
BUT ON THE
VERY LAST

NOT ON THE LAST DAY, BUT ON THE VERY LAST

| POEMS |

JUSTIN BOENING

MILKWEED EDITIONS

Published 2016 by Milkweed Editions
Printed in the United States of America
Cover design by Gretchen Achilles
Cover illustration by Ekely / Getty Images
Author photo by Devon Walker-Figueroa
16 17 18 19 20   5 4 3 2 1
FIRST EDITION

Milkweed Editions, an independent nonprofit publisher, gratefully acknowledges sustaining support
from the Jerome Foundation; the Lindquist & Vennum Foundation; the McKnight Foundation; the
National Endowment for the Arts; the Target Foundation; and other generous contributions from foun-
dations, corporations, and individuals. Also, this activity is made possible by the voters of Minnesota
through a Minnesota State Arts Board Operating Support grant, thanks to a legislative appropriation
from the arts and cultural heritage fund, and a grant from the Wells Fargo Foundation Minnesota. For a
full listing of Milkweed Editions supporters, please visit www.milkweed.org.

Library of Congress Cataloging-in-Publication Data

Names: Boening, Justin, author.
Title: Not on the last day, but on the very last : poems / Justin Boening.
Description: Minneapolis, Minnesota : Milkweed Editions, 2016.
Identifiers: LCCN 2016013643 (print) | LCCN 2016014063 (ebook) | ISBN
9781571314871 (paperback) | ISBN 9781571319517 (e-book)
Subjects: | BISAC: POETRY / American / General.
Classification: LCC PS3602.O42274 A6 2016 (print) | LCC PS3602.O42274 (ebook)
| DDC 811/.6--dc23
LC record available at http://lccn.loc.gov/2016013643

Milkweed Editions is committed to ecological stewardship. We strive to align our book production
practices with this principle, and to reduce the impact of our operations in the environment. We are a
member of the Green Press Initiative, a nonprofit coalition of publishers, manufacturers, and authors
working to protect the world's endangered forests and conserve natural resources. *Not on the Last Day,
but on the Very Last* was printed on acid-free 100% postconsumer-waste paper by Edwards Brothers
Malloy.

CONTENTS

ONE

TWO

THREE

ONE

The wind is having its way with the house tonight,
with the windows.
                    It's finally possible

to undress myself like a Corinthian. I remove
the crickets
                    from my pillow, place the clock

facedown, lay my brass collar stays
in a leather box.
                    It's my turn to suffer.

The stovepipe gnaws through the room like an emperor
who's lost his voice,
                    and you're at it again,

burning laps in the ambulance
out on the frozen lake.
                    Everything seems

like something you'd say to me
                                in a small town
to keep me breathing like a little beast—

skein of brant breaking heavy, some cut-loose
kindling. Neither of us
                    has been perfect.

I carry my fistful of pebbles,
you still threaten to swallow them down

when I'm distracted, lost
in a squall of chrysanthemums

and the weird. Place the world
                                back in orbit—
I was mistaken. If you do not

come closer, we will not
                        need our umbrage.
It is not snow that covers us,

nor spooks, nor wind, just as
                                this isn't a shadow
(say stranger), or the carrying off

of one animal in place of another.

TO BE A GOD

Starting now, I'll do everything
                                    as if I were a god.

I'll walk from a dark room
                                    as a god walks from a dark room.

I'll speak to strangers
                                    as a god speaks to strangers.

When it's time to say something important

I'll rise from my chair
                                    as a god would
                and speak in my

                                    celestial certitudes.

There will be no more
                                    lap-sitting,

                no more stories
                                    about my days
as a barback or a ferryman

or a farrier.
                                    There will be fewer hours spent tuning
my piano
                and patting my hunting dogs
or remembering
                                    my youth. When I need you to hurt

I'll put you to sleep as a god puts you to sleep,

I'll play my discordant harp as a god plays a harp,

and the effects will be the same.

The noise of the bramble
                    never leaves me.

I bless the cedar. The months go by. I bless your saw.

When you need
                    me to hurt, I'll dim

in the linden leaves, I'll hide
                              in the fire-scarred hills,

and the great guards
                    of my gilded name

will circle around to protect me.
                              And you'll be there,

and I'll know your name
                    as a god knows your name,
as a father knows your name,
                    but you won't recognize me.

MY MOTHER TAKES THE STAND

The room is walking
                          into a woman. It's lying to you
again—hasn't learned.   .

The room is walking into a woman and he claims
                                                    this time
he has the evidence. A telephone

dangles from his white-collar neck. Right.

That's my cue.

              Is it acceptable if I repeat myself?

I scan the radio, hear nothing
                          good. I argue my side like a child
crying down the dead limbs

of a backyard tree. The room
                          closes its doors, wanting to rest
its eyes a little, and I open them back up.

No. A man on the side of a road
                          swaddled an infant and waved a flare.

No. In the field a prop plane
                          was burning the field, was yelling
at the sky.

Yes. In a muggy room a woman,
        with the blinds clacking in a breeze, with the television
talking buzz on mute, packed a suitcase,
                        a photograph on top, and every word
heard in the room
                        was an afterlife? The room became dumbly
an afterlife? This was her way

of apologizing. This was her way
                        of sending me threats. Who
can avoid falling in love
        with a good lie. Who the hell do you think you are?

ON THE MYSTERIOUS DISAPPEARANCE
OF FORTUNETELLERS

Desire is a failure
                    to frighten oneself
out of the home.

                    I have no desire. My mother
kept a tape recorder
                    propped by a sloop

in a bottle. They both burned
                              in a fire I started
with her books, the family books,

after she'd told me of the man
                              I'd become. It's funny
what people do for money.

In a waiting room, a doctor lifts a needle
                              from a record,
says my name like he's heard his wife say it

in passing. In his office
                    he assures me that though
I think I love ugly

people, I only truly love
                    myself. He asks about my mother.

They always ask
                about my mother. I tell him,
There should be a rule

against inheritance. He shakes
                        his head. He shoves
        a black-and-white photo

below my nose: a scrawny
                jungle cat, neck bent,
lapping mud water

from a puddle. I flip the photo over
                        and write this
note to myself for later: *Thank god*
                        our kind hasn't yet died off.

SELF-PORTRAIT IN WHICH I RESEMBLE THE MAN NEXT TO ME

When nobody's watching
                            I lose my lisp,
gape my mouth,
                  eat my teeth
back in, like an engine running
                       through the night.

This isn't new to me:
                     the knife on my white
tongue, like a pill,
                rolled scarf stuffed
down my throat, me
                  wearing nothing
but this dumb

hat. Could you hold this,
                   this book, through winters?
Through winters,
            I'll write you letters
in it, on my knees, on my face—
                 I'll not say a thing

until I'm certain.
              To save myself,
I remove myself. My voice
               is waking me. I want it
to wake me again.

NOBODY

When you find me a wreck,
                    curled in weird flowers,
don't wake me; tell nobody I'm here,

that you love me because you love anyone
                    who plans to leave you, that the lies
you've used against me are different

from the lies you've used against yourself,
                    that by remaining here, unthinkably still,
we'll be moving closer to the mountains

we've always wanted to be
                    (the ones that wear disguises),
that nobody gifted us this sad

talent, that if our eyes were windows,
                    they were also mirrors reflecting back
nobody's ineffable vanity,

that nobody is who we send when we send
                    our apologies, that nobody has written
the ending we want for ourselves.

THE JUKEBOX THAT ENDED THE WORLD TWICE

There are many predictions
                              about how the world will end,
and I believe them all.

The priests are planning a party
                              in the rectory.

The children are drawing hopscotch

on truck beds. I'm running a bath
                              and lighting
vanilla candles. I'm thinking

of playing the guitar
                              badly. In one scenario
I sweat to death reclined

in my living room chair.
                              In another, I choke
on ash, splayed out

on the peeling linoleum.
                              But in another (and this one's
my favorite), the planet's thin crust pries

from its mantle,
                    the magnetic poles switch places
like a boy

twisting a muddy ball cap
                                 around his doughy head.
The continents,

they learn to whistle
                    like locusts—it has happened before.
In preparation, I begin

on my bed writing these letters
                                 back to you: *Forget the snow*
that doesn't fall. Father no children.

PROXY BAPTISM

It happens each day.
                                  Black water scallops—
an obsidian. I begin

to count backward
                            in a dory,
           a duffle coat

draped stiff
                    from my shoulders.
I'm unsure

of what I'll do, the lake
                          of blue petals
becoming. Over the bow

my fingers
                  brush waters,
leave small wakes.

I make a mess of things.
                          A bird sings
from the bank

like a needle.
                    A speck of gravel
lodges like a pit

in my throat. Willow
                    juts through my teeth
like bees, and I forget

my body, my hands,
                    like an argument,
while at the river's edge,

a family clutches candles
                    close to their moonlit
nightgowns, they whisper

when they turn from me,
                    as I empty
past them, as I try to tell them

the war is over
                    (though it isn't),
and I shake myself

to wake a deer bent down
                    inside of me
and I'm alone. I believe

I'm alone
            when I'm alone.
I cannot move,

and a woman
            is taking my hair.

THE OPERA SINGER

My mother picked me
                    from a lineup, ill-shaven, sick
to my stomach. She caught me ravaging

a nunnery's pantry
                    for chocolate coins.

Her assistant, the injured
                    ballroom dancer, says
she travels the countryside
                    for the kind of talent

a train yard is born with.
                    He says the boy
in front of you's
                    got it to spare.

They brought me here
                    without my props,
I take my time,

keep my eye
                    on the audience, I find my place.
A young man

in the orchestra seats
                    cleans his wire-rim glasses.
A pigeon bolts
                    from the folds of a dusty curtain,

lands like a broken faucet
                        on a woman's
wicker hat. I crack
                my knuckles

on my jaw, lick my hand
                        to groom my hair.
There's a moment
                when I'm meant to sing,

when the music
                slows, after the overture,

after a paper horse trots
                        my costar into a cellophane field,

and I'm ready (why am I afraid?),
                                I'm ready

and the paper horse
                        trots into the cellophane field

which is when I begin, only
                        out of turn, and the notes
jangle. Back in the dressing room,

my mother paces
                in the mirror, fills the air
with smoke. She tells me

she doesn't eat
                enough meat.

Before she sends me
                    back to the stage,
she strokes my hand, says,

"A painting grows
                    more modern
like a weakness,"

watches me dress myself
                    in a costume plucked
from her brass-trim trunk—

velvet bolero, long
                    white gloves, one
wing tip boot.

It doesn't look right,
                    but the audience loves it
when I clear my throat,

when I raise my hand. When I start to sing

TWO

THE BANQUET

It was confusing, at first,
                              entering the banquet,
strange that though I was only a boy, my body
was already repulsive. The dented kitchen doors
swinging open as if by themselves, the room's
emaciated laughter
                              coming to a sudden end.
And wouldn't you know it, that was the moment
I saw it—the fold-up chair someone
had forgotten in the center of the dance floor,
as if just for me.
                         I wrestled myself
to the top of it, thrust my arms out to the side
to find my balance. I scanned over the tables,
over the flickering orange faces of the feasters,
and, knowing what they wanted, or at least
believing I did, I opened the book
I carry with me
                         to its final few pages.
A man wearing a monocle leapt to his feet,
rapping a cake fork on the side of an empty glass.
I coughed into my fist, and an underfed busboy
lost a whole tray of chardonnay. I shook my head
in disbelief, I smiled and said,
                              "Stay calm, my children.
I've heard that somewhere. The world as it is
is only the world as it might be."
"How true," said one guest, as she began to cry.
"How expected," muttered another.
But yes, I could hear what you were saying, too.

I'd been you before.
                    So tell me, you sirs and madams,
after all the topaz candlelight and windblown
afternoons, after all the glamorous toasts
and dancing and withering away,
                                does sadness leave us?
Is that the source of sadness?

THE MISTAKE

You and I have likely a very different understanding of why
we've made the mistake of coming here, of journeying
all this way, by which I mean peering through the window
of this one-room cabin, called *now* or *earth* or *love*, just to sprawl
our tired limbs on a stranger's
                                    disturbingly beige carpet.
Nevertheless, I often find myself wondering about
the not-so-innocent lives of oil paintings,
the awfully blue horses kneeling in their shade,
the way their impossible green goes on living, never standing
a chance of learning how awkwardly similar they are
                                                        to us.
And I forget us, as this snow is forgetting this streetlamp,
these power lines, as these unsuspecting farmers rust
in their fields and never know they were part of something
too important to see, a part of time, which is
a part of me, a form of struggle
                                    itself becoming
struggle, and ending in a courage to surrender to a will
remarkably not one's own—a shock of crows lifting
from the hand of a tree, or a tree lifting from the hand
                                    of no one you know.

ILLNESS

You let go of my sleeve.
　　　　　　I told you not to.
You snatched at the black wire bent
　　　　　　in the shape of a bird.

The branch chatter hummed
　　　like machines in your breath.
You were the child's carriage choked
　　　　with soiled linens on the lawn.

The neighbors are loud.
　　　　The season, like the hour,
like whatever it is
　　　　　you're waiting for, is almost

ready to leave, almost bon voyage,
　　　　　up for grabs; you should forget
your familiar promises—
　　　　　　there's little you can do.

Illness lets you know it's coming
　　　　　　by not saying a word. It wants
and wants like the ribs of a mule,
　　　　　　like the hands of a child,

it barges through the doors
　　　　　　without showing its face,
without flashing a badge—
　　　　　　it knows no one
by knowing more than you.

IDIOM OF THE ENTREPRENEUR

If I have to. If you go back
                    to the beach hotel
without me. If the birds

against the sun turn
                    to sun, and the idea

of solitude no longer
          dithers on the radio.
If I become wild again

and no longer respond
                    to my name. Don't

be alarmed. I have
                    possession of pyramids.
I own farms by product.

There's room for me here,
          if there's room for me here

also. If, in an empty church,
                    a muted light gifts
a spontaneous world.

If the candles aren't
                    meant for you,

they're meant for you,
                    they have their say,
though you rarely hear it.

Then I lie down. Then
                    I believe again
in a lamppost

that doesn't believe in me.
                    Farewell to phone calls,
to matchbooks. I've said it all,

if I've moved
                    my belongings. The bed
is empty—nothing to see here.

THEN AFTER

Then after I finished, after the pegs were good
and in the ground, I stayed
under the empty circus tent, and I sat like a nail
at the edge of the center ring. I didn't know
what to say. Hours passed. I sat there. Then
out of nowhere
                        a lioness entered the ring.
And with my hands on her waist, her claws
shining on my shoulders, we forgot the dance
we'd meant to dance,
                        but we danced,
kicked circles in the sod, imagined the children,
the families, all filling the vacant bleachers,
the ringmaster lifting a bullhorn
to his wretched mouth.
                        We would have taken a bow
in the spotlight had a spotlight
                        been shining on us,
but we were glad to be rid of ourselves,
even for a moment, glad to dance the dance
that made our irrelevance
                        more real, though our limbs
lacked grace, especially mine, or maybe it was the dance
itself that lacked grace.
                        But we were glad to be part
of the show, or part of the dance whose primitive
lunges and flailing we repeated, and though
the swaying couldn't be our own, though
we would have never thought to move this way,

we kept dancing.
                              We heard the loose sound
of a church bell whose cargo jangled each night
through the streets, and after that, the far-off
celebration of wolves or dogs or freaks
wafting through the grass.
                              We'd meant to dance
forever. That's what we'd meant to do.
But the lioness was getting tired,
                              or I was,
and the dance started to feel
less like a dance and more like a language.
And the lioness looked up at me, with a tear
falling from her massive amber eye, and said,
"This is it, you know.
We won't be getting a second chance."

ELECTION DAY

It began
          with the belief
(foolishly misguided)

that the slaves
               hadn't learned
how to talk,

that they didn't
               know, couldn't
know, that

what they longed for
                    (as did all of us)
was the cold satisfaction

of assembling, just
               for the pleasure

of tearing apart. It was
               election day.

We were electing
               our replacements. A voice

from the mob
          rose above it,
shouting, "Here they come!"

and then
                    "The soldiers! The soldiers!"

We all put down
                    our ballots, tearfully
applauding, imagining

the distant battles,
                    dusty mountains,

how the beginning
                    of war is always
a myth, just as its end,

how even the present
                    is unrecognizable
as it leaves you.

One of the men
                    waved a twisted branch

that stuck from his cuff
                    in place of a hand;

another, as a gesture
                    of generosity,
          pried open

his mouth until
                    it turned
     into a cave,

so all of us
        who were there
    by choice

(and our children
            too) could hear
each other's voices

inside him: hesitant,
                sorrowful,
        diminishing.

TWO SURGEONS

It was a snowy night in March.
I had little to do.
So I signed myself
into the ER,
took a penknife from my jacket
pocket, and cut into the chest
of a sweet old man
who was clutching his heart
in the sweaty leather chair next to mine.

Two surgeons, hearing
the man's inhuman cries,
pushed aside a pack of nurses,
vaulted over a counter,
and knelt beside me
to hold open my incisions.

I should have expected
this day would come.
Everyone always told me
I was meant for greatness.

In the corner, a girl
snipped eyelashes
from her baby doll. A boy
creased asthma pamphlets
into unflyable paper machines.
Every once in a while,
the doctors would dart glances
at one another, as if they might be

trying to say something specific
like "Incredible," or "I haven't
seen it done like this in years."

I felt persecuted. I felt the need
to retort: I said, "Fashion, gentlemen,
is for those without style."

The two surgeons must have sensed
how furious they'd made me.
They dropped their bloody instruments
to the carpet, raised their gloved
hands in the air, and began
slowly to back away.

That's when it occurred to me
(I think it was then) that these
two men and I had met before,
long ago, perhaps in an age of kings,
when I myself was king. They may
have even been forced to attend
one of my weddings, or served me lamb
while I lounged on a chaise in my silk
paisley pajamas, because back then,
in that sand-strewn time, when
our apathy was surpassed only
by our unwillingness to change,
we changed our laws as often
as our laws allowed.

THE DINER

There's a man who's been waiting
in that red vinyl booth
for days. I've tried to ignore him
from behind my giant notepad,
but in the morning, barely able
to stand, I demand he tells me
how he takes his eggs.
He doesn't move.

I pour a pot of hot coffee
straight into his lap. I start chanting
my college fight song
and pawing down all the blinds.
I press a butter knife
to my throat, throw an order of hash
against the wall. Once and for all
I prove unemployable.

When it becomes clear
he won't be convinced,
I pull the net from my tangled hair
and shuffle, slouched, into the farthest
corner in the place. I hide my face
behind a glossy menu. I close my eyes
and in no time I'm alone.
I hear people come, people go.
From time to time, I glance
out the window, toward the traffic
buzzing by, hoping my waitress
might visit my table soon. Sometimes,

I sense I'm being spoken to
or scolded, while other times
I hear a woman crying, a car door
clicking open, then slamming shut,
a motorcycle revving alive,
then veering into traffic, but it seems
little ever truly changes, and I've been
waiting here, with the rest of you,
hungry for years.

At the base of the lobby stairs,
you comb your hair in the mirror,
tap a bell, and call down a dim corridor:
"Show yourself, you coward!"

You hear a moan. Then a yawn.
Then, peeking from behind
a massive marble column,
you spot a bony man unbuttoning,
then buttoning his shirt,
slowly closing the mahogany cover
over the keys of a player piano,
his neck nearly swallowed whole
by a blue padded polyester suit.

"Thank you," he sighs, looking up,
a bellboy cap tilting into his eyes.
"After all these years of pretending,
I finally feel ready to serve again."

He grunts as he heaves your trunk
to the sharp knob of his shoulder
and takes the first velvet step
on the long climb up the stairs.

"But Father—"

"I'm not your father," he says,
"and haven't been for some time.
Now let me show you your room.
Everything is as you left it."

It'll be funny

      knowing for once they won't be singing to me forever,
like hearing a woman's voice

      walking farther and farther into an empty field
wearing a stranger's coat;

and forgetting, of course,

      because by then their cruel music will have stopped,
that woman in the foyer

      buttoning and unbuttoning my shirt, trying on
all of my winter hats,

when, as the sky went motionless, then dark, then loud

      and precise, everyone at the party
covered their mouths, covered their eyes, and the mutt

      sitting at my feet started to hum, started to froth,
which is to say the wine became unbearably sweet,

      and the crack in the front door
grew longer, not wider;

and realizing, also,

      what I'd always known to be the case, that I wanted to believe
I could finally walk on the brink

      of my body, but didn't know if belief
was the right response,

      that I wanted to kiss each of my guests
on the cheek as they left

      with the lights on;

and, especially then,

                    scooping the fallen ash as if it were snow,
to lift just some of what was left
                    to your tongue;

and trying to recall
                just what it was that had gone
so completely right, or why it is
                  the way I leave you
      is over and over again.

THE KIND OF LIFE I ALWAYS WANTED

I've finished what I set out to,
                                   given up
on desire, preferring the silent

commerce of unwinding wire
                                   from a spool,
and I've celebrated your sadness

like a child hiding
                       underneath a boathouse,
called catastrophe a horse

that waited for me to ride him,
                                   too tired to pull
at his mane. I'm a fool.

Or at least aloof. And yet
                             I've come this far,
which, I've been assured,

is far enough. The pickup
                             is burning gas,
I have no place to go.

I'm unpacking my luggage
                             and have no reason
to stay. This kind of life

is the kind of life I always wanted:

                          little is recorded,

little remembered long. It has

little to share, little to give,

                 and an abundance

it's willing to part with.

It has nothing to say,

               no excuse for staying quiet.

THE DOOR

In the wilderness, a door
           stands upright. Its paint
peeling, its knob

a little loose. I place a palm
           of dead bees beside it
to remind the trees

of what it is
           to be young. There's more
to being human

than painting pictures
           of birds as they return
back home to us.

A mother who sleeps
           without a blanket, like a cat
curled on a dock, walks back

to her cold house
           cradling a child's
toy horse. The women

around her weep
           until they remember
they are women.

Suppose the worst happens,
                    the door opens,
and a hundred white moths

flicker into a blue
                    improbable night.
This story is not the story

I'll tell my children,
                    but more like a bowl
of water divided into bowls,

more like tilting
                    porcelain stacked
in a sink.

We find the door
                    by moonlight, gather rugs,
carry our tired bodies to it,

and take turns saying
                    "I pass every man
on the road to his village."

Every time I stand before it
                    I imagine
a better conclusion.

Every time I open the door
                    there's another child
we call wolf.

THREE

FIELD KABUKI

I see so little
            these days, I think
I must be alive.

And yet these leaves
                go clattering.
And yet these leaves.

Please accept
            our sincerest
apologies, they say.

A blade of grass
                that thought
it was a tree and was right.

Is there another world?
                        Is it this one?

Is there another world?
                        Is it this one?

THE GAME

It's late. The hero has returned—
unhelpful as ever. He's hiding out
in the neighbor's orchard,
steering clear of the constable.
The citizens have left empty
all the houses, all the shops—
the screen doors hollow on hinges,
a porch swing hinging by a chain.

I'm on my way out of town
with a dog-eared bible
and a leather valise. The time,
if we're being honest,
just seems right. I stand
over the fence gate,
where it used to be.
I try to remember the sound
it made when I'd let go of it.
I ask the constable,
"Do you have the time?"
but he doesn't understand
the question. The children
dancing in the street
answer for him with a song:
"11:30, 2:00 a.m., midnight, sir,
too late for you," and I realize
it's so much earlier than I'd thought,
that I have all the time in the world
and will need every minute.

But where will I go?
Or where have I gone?
And where did the boy
who slept for days outside
his house go? I've lived
in this town all my life,
and still the roads quarreling
in its outskirts
are mysterious to me,
one unanswered question
after another, inflating this world
into the next. I cry out

to the boy: "Boy, this town
has nothing to offer me anymore—
Why am I still so afraid
to leave it?" The slow hours
churning in its streets. The record
the wind keeps of this moment
becoming the wind keeping a record
of what's to come,

and in this wind the boy
says to me, "Listen,
if you walk west, over those
blue hills, through those
marshes of lost horses, and you just
keep going, keep walking, over those
trees that are lying down, into that
light that's standing up, you'll become
the west, which is just a direction,
and nothing could be more cruel."

The boy looks up at me, charcoal eyes,
clearly waiting to hear me say
exactly the words he's been longing
to hear all his life, the promise

that one's love turns into a poem
by the end, that the people
we grieve for come back,
that some voice, however small,
from some wave
receding into waves, finally tells us
there was no particular way
it was meant to happen,
that every mistake one makes
one makes through his own attempt
to be fathomed.

"You've lost," I say.
"But only out here," says the boy,
"in this town's dusty reaches,
where there are no games to lose,
and no one to console you
if there were." "No," I say,
"you've lost in this place
because there is no other.
I'm leaving you now
to spread the good news."

THE VERY VERY IMPORTANT BENEFACTOR

Every evening for these past five days,
               the elderly woman who whistles
in the garden behind my house
        gallops into my room to strangle me.

It's fun at first. We bay the most
               abhorrent jibes as she breaches
my boudoir: "Prince!" "Not prince!"

I hurl a hammer, then my heaviest
               books, at her breasts, her bony face,
before she backs away, takes a bow,
               only to barrel down on my throat.

She's no one I've ever known. I want
               to call her "Whale" or worse,
a witch with an arrow through her heart,

but I won't. "Weakling," I wheeze while I wince
        under her black grip; the word "Suffer" arrives
with a fork, a needling at my tongue; "Charlatan,"
               she whimpers with a mouthful of ash

and crackers; "Fair enough, bad mother,"
        I bicker. "Forgive me" doesn't mean we end,
but we end soon after. Back in the garden,

lounging in my linen hammock, the hag
               moans, "I miss you, my bastard."
Why have I made it so difficult to love you?

THE STORY AS IT WAS TOLD TO ME

This is the new story, new
                        and accidental: praise

for a woman who falls asleep in a field, behaves

like the moon,
                   for the stars, how they no longer tell me
to feel warm

or wrong. It goes on and on:
                      a woman wakes

in the dead center of a dry field.
                       A man and his dog
rustle like hatchets through its husks.

The woman cannot see them
                       rushing closer, clawing stalks,
but hears the man's voice
                 calling, "I miss you,
come to bed,"
          again and again,

but none of it's true.

               You've heard this story too:
no rain, no noon light
            indifferent in it,

no hours falling
           to a kitchen floor.

It's the story you tell yourself
           when you're waiting,

patiently wanting nothing to happen, nothing
                       you've prepared for
or believed could ever come, something

like the day you entered
           the house you owned

by not owning a house, something
                       like speaking to the father
you love by not loving one.

THE PORTRAIT OF WHAT IS NOT THERE

I'm tired of painting the portrait of what is not there.
And I should be. The way it is, the way it has to be,
the portrait of what is not there seems too narcissistic
to ever be complete.
                    I brush and scratch and know
the landscape so well—the noiseless trees,
the insentient breezes that are not there—
it's almost as if I were part of it. And yet
I manage to imagine only patches of it at a time:
a canyon that would attempt to constrict before me
if it were there to constrict before me;
a talus slope failing to glitter under that strange dish,
the moon; a few pencil-thin birds ceaselessly drifting
through a pink sky I see is there
                              when it can be anything
but there. The portrait of what is not there
is one of many things I can't stand about me. I tell myself
the painted lakes will become brighter when the light
from my body enters into them. I tell myself
there's more to this place than what the portrait
can make me believe. If only there were a portrait
of what is not there, in the portrait of what is not there.
If only I could live in its night, under the color
of that strange dish, I might continue painting
what's not there, letting *here*
                              alone. And the portrait
of what is not there would hang in the museum
of what is not there. And I'd no longer be painting the portrait,
but living it. And I'd see life, but not this one.

It ends like a lightbulb
                     in an empty room,
having a body. The way I feel

isn't interesting anymore.
                          Through the window,
a chemical, ripe as silk,

quarrels in the burn of surf.
                       A child on the beach
loses her black

ribbon house. I will go on
                    as long as there are mirrors.
A horse kicks limp straw

in a paddock. I soothe her hair
                     with a stiff wire brush. An ocean
approaches the door. The outline

of a man, man of small lights, mingles with dirt
                                    as it jolts
from her encrusted mane. My watch is wrong,

I shake it. The grasses grow strange.
                       When I say I
I mean the things I do. It's time
                       I start telling the truth.

NOBODY

after Mark Levine

Yesterday was nobody's favorite day, but it's almost over.
Nobody was dancing naked on a truck idling in a driveway.
Nobody was dancing with a woman who wasn't there.
Nobody was claiming his life was just a metaphor
for founding a town. Nobody was knocking back whiskey.
Nobody lacked remorse.

                    And on an old highway,
macadam, long decommissioned, that used to host
caravans of families going to church, I bumped
into a boy who swore to me he
was my son. I kissed him on the head,
told him, "Don't run off like that."

"This is the saddest moment of my life," I said.
"This is the saddest moment of nobody's life," he said.

And as we pushed aside a tangle of leaves to enter
a stolen wood, we knew we'd be joined
by no one dragging their empty bags behind them.
And the poplars began to shake, or we did.
And the leaves reflected light as they twisted
in a dumb wind—a school of fish
shot through by sun—and nobody was bothered
by a reality that had already come, and nobody
was longing for the one that hadn't.

HOW I CAME TO RULE THE WORLD

First, no one loved me. Then
I learned to love myself
too much. The rest, as they say,
is the rest.
        I ran and ran
for what seemed like months,
for what seemed like days
without nights, without sleep,
through stampedes of others
dressed up to look just like me—
what I took to be the infernos
I'd been promised
and had always dreamed of.
I prayed for the lord
               to take me
until he did. And before
I could realize that I was doing it
all wrong, I found myself
at the edge of an abandoned city,
and I said to myself
             "This is it,"
and the wind swelled,
so I pulled off a boot,
and then some fog dissolved,
so I unbuttoned my shirt,
and when nothing more
could be removed, when
nothing more could be
left behind, I stood up,
wearing nothing but a scarf, and began

again to walk, this time toward
the glowing center of the city, a piazza
of black marble and bare-
limbed trees, white, growing
like wire from the marble,
and there emerged, in bronze
curves, oxidized, flaked
in mint lichen, right there
. within the muggy vicinity,
a statue of me.
            And I wept
beneath it on my knees, relieved
at its being there, but mostly
exhausted from the punishment—
and that was it. How I came
to rule the world? It was easy.

AS YOU LEFT IT

It would have been hilarious
had they allowed me to live
forever, paying in divine wisdom
for all my erotic massages,
tipping the jazz quartet
with whatever cocktail coaster
I'd scribbled on the night before,

but it's even stranger here,
now, feeling the cool air
as the concierge kicks me
through the kitchen's
steel back doors, the cruise ship
shoving off from the dock
without me, into the moon-
pocked waves, the stubborn mists,
anything as meaningless
and impossible to imagine as us,

and in the end what drives me nuts
is knowing what I never
thought possible—that when
one returns to his body,
his body will be as he left it,
meaning nakedness on a man
is always a comedy—
and wondering not whether
they'll have me back
but why, and who will be there
waiting to forgive me
for giving up again.

ACKNOWLEDGMENTS

The Atlas Review: "On the Mysterious Disappearance of Fortunetellers"

Boston Review: "To Be a God" and "Then After"

The Collagist: "Self-Portrait in Which I Resemble the Man next to Me"

Colorado Review: "Proxy Baptism"

Columbia: A Journal of Literature and Art: "Idiom of the Entrepreneur"

Copper Nickel: "Nobody" and "As You Left It"

Denver Quarterly: "Field Kabuki"

Fiddleback: "The Jukebox That Ended the World Twice" and "The Opera
    Singer"

Fruita Pulp: "Player Piano"

The Journal: "The Story as It Was Told to Me"

Kenyon Review Online: "How I Came to Rule the World"

Linebreak: "When I Cannot Sleep—Day Six—a Letter"

Los Angeles Review of Books Quarterly: "The Banquet"

Miami Rail: "My Mother Takes the Stand" and "When the Buskers Leave
    Town for Good"

Narrative: "Two Surgeons" and "The Portrait of What Is Not There"

Nashville Review: "The Diner"

Phantom Limb: "The Door"

Pinwheel: "The Mistake" and "Nobody"

Saint Ann's Review: "The Very Very Important Benefactor"

Sixth Finch: "Habeas Corpus"

Third Coast: "Illness"

TYPO: "Election Day"

Women's Studies Quarterly: "The Kind of Life I Always Wanted"

I'd also like to offer special thanks to the Poetry Society of America for publishing a number of these poems in a chapbook, *Self-Portrait as Missing Person*; Tupelo Press for selecting "How I Came to Rule the World" for their *30/30 Anthology*; and *Verse Daily* for featuring "When I Cannot Sleep—Day Six—a Letter" as part of their web feature.

DEVON WALKER-FIGUEROA

JUSTIN BOENING is the author of *Self-Portrait as Missing Person*, which was awarded a Poetry Society of America National Chapbook Fellowship. He is a recipient of the "Discovery"/*Boston Review* Poetry Prize, a work-study scholarship from the Bread Loaf Writers' Conference, a Stadler Fellowship from Bucknell University, and a Henry David Thoreau Fellowship from the Vermont Studio Center. His poetry and reviews have appeared or are forthcoming in a variety of publications such as *Denver Quarterly*, *Kenyon Review Online*, *Los Angeles Review of Books Quarterly Journal*, *Narrative*, and *TYPO*, among others. Boening is currently a senior editor at *Poetry Northwest*, and is cofounding editor at Horsethief Books.

Interior design by Gretchen Achilles / Wavetrap Design
Typeset in Bembo
by Gretchen Achilles / Wavetrap Design

Bembo was designed in 1496 by Francesco Griffo, and later adapted by Stanley Morison at Monotype in 1929. It is a classic humanist type known for its elegant roman weights and graceful italics.